YORK C
Walk...g ....

THE MINOR PLEASURES
OF YORK

By Dr. John Shannon, O.B.E., D. Univ. (YORK)

YORK CIVIC TRUST

The York Civic Trust Walking Guides
are published by Maxiprint, York, England.

Series editor: Peter B Brown

Walking instructions are given in red type. This route is also
suitable for pushchairs and wheelchairs.

Supplementary information is provided in these green
panels and can, if so wished, be read in conjunction with
the main text.

York Civic Trust
Walking Guide
The Minor Pleasures of York
ISBN: 1 871125 06 5

All the photographs are by the author.
Numbers 13A and 28A are reproduced with the permission of
the Dean and Chapter of York Minster and York City Council
respectively.

Front cover: Minerva, Godesss of Wisdom and Drama, to be
seen on the corner of Minster Gates.

To most people, visitor and citizen alike, the name York conjures up a picture of the Minster, Bar Walls, Guildhalls and the other principal buildings of the city. But one of the attractions of York is the general fabric of the city which forms, as it were, the backcloth to the great monuments. It is in itself a fascinating mixture of the architectural styles of all ages, and just as a very good picture requires a frame equally as good in its own right, so does the general fabric of the city set off and complement the great architecture we observe. And it contains a wealth of detail - what I call The Minor Pleasures of York.

Come with me and let me share them with you. Remember there will be many distractions to draw you away from the path I have chosen, but those delights can be saved for another day.

John Shannon

1993

The Mansion House built c.1725 - 32 and modelled on the Queen's Gallery at Somerset House, London, designed by Inigo Jones. It is the residence of the Right Honourable The Lord Mayor of York during his year of office.

The Mansion House is one of York's finest Georgian buildings, but the interesting thing is that though it was the City Council which built it, nobody to this day knows who the architect was. Many guesses are made and the best guess might be that it was by a man called William Etty.

The Arms of the City are unique. Although very old, they were confirmed by the Office of Heralds in 14th century and there is no Coat of Arms in England like them.

The Lord Mayor of York is second only to the Lord Mayor of London and only upon him and the capital cities of the United Kingdom and Glasgow is conferred the right to use the title Right Honourable.

The pediment of The Mansion House showing the Coat of Arms of the City of York: the five lions of England upon the cross of St. George.

and here yet another lion, **the Knocker** on the front door (almost polished out of existence).

The Lamp Standards surmounted by the same lion,

Looking to the right, observe the fine Italianate building, formerly the home of the Yorkshire Insurance Company (1840)

Terry's Shop which you will also see is now a retail shop with the Trustee Savings Bank above it.

It was one of the best shops and restaurants in York until the Americans, who took over Terry's for a brief span, closed it down. More fools they. But all the original mahogany panelling remains and is now listed. It is well worth while taking a glance inside. The panelling in what was Terry's restaurant upstairs and behind the present shop is very redolent of the old transatlantic liners, and indeed it came to York as a result of a cancelled order for such a liner.

The Trustee Savings Bank with its attractive lettering above.

The splendid railings (very masculine as compared with the more delicate ones round The Mansion House).

and across the street

An impresive cast iron entrance to the Lakeland shop.

The railings both here and on the front of the old Yorkshire Insurance Building are two examples of many which are a feature of York. It is in fact quite remarkable that so many good railings survived two world wars and were not taken to help the war effort.

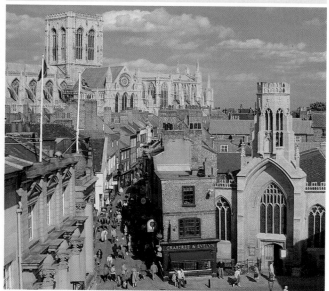

Stonegate a highway for nearly 2,000 years and one of York's
finest streets, containing as it does the architecture of all ages
from Norman to Victorian.

Wander down this street noticing as you go on the left

The jettied building faced with Minton tiles, (although
behind them lies a timbered mediaeval building).

A little further on the right

A ship's figurehead as the main feature of this timbered
mediaeval building. What is a ship's figurehead doing in the
middle of an inland mediaeval city?

Stonegate into which you have moved owes its name to the
fact that it was once a stone paved street and not, as is
commonly said, because the stone to build York Minster was
brought along here from the river behind the Mansion House -
although it was. It is almost a perfect townscape with
buildings from the Norman to late Victorian eras, and all living
happily together.

7

GUY FAWKES

Hereabouts lived the parents of Guy Fawkes of Gunpowder Plot fame; who was baptized in St. Michael-le-Belfrey Church in 1570.

A Civic Trust plaque concerning the birthplace of Guy Fawkes (whatever you may read later on in our walk).

Cross the street and look out for a passageway bounded by some charming gates. Proceed to the top of the 'ginnel'.

The York Medical Society rooms and **the earliest rainwater head in York .** The Society was founded in 1832.

Retrace your steps and turn right towards Coffee Yard.

A Little Red Devil chained round his middle. A sensible precaution after seeing the ship's figurehead?

A small diversion into Coffee Yard will repay the effort. York Archaeological Trust's impressive restoration of Barley Hall and adjoining coffee house gives a real insight into aspects of mediaeval and Georgian York. The coffee and Fat Rascals are good too.

Barley Hall c.1485 thought to have been a monastic hospice belonging to Nostell Priory near Wakefield.

Return to the street and on the right

What is thought to be a Dutch coat of Arms above an impressive Georgian shop façade.

Carry on to the junction

Many of York's buildings which have Victorian or Georgian façades have timbered structures behind and many of them are in fact ships' timbers, because when York's role as a port declined, the laid up ships on the quaysides formed a ready source of building material and this is no doubt the explanation for the ship's figurehead. The street was originally a road leading to the Roman legionary headquarters under where the Minster is now, (the remains of which can be seen in the foundations). It was the Roman *Via Praetoria*.

A carving of **Minerva, the Goddess of Wisdom and Drama** on the corner of Minster Gates

Notice on the left **a Sign outside Young's Hotel** proclaiming that it was the birth-place of Guy Fawkes (which it never was - remember?)

Proceed across the junction towards Bootham Bar (Don't be tempted by the Minster just yet, this comes a little later). Notice the Fire Mark high up on the left near Bootham Bar

An attractive **Insurance Fire Mark** the Royal company was founded in 1845, keep your eyes open for more of these and other Fire Marks on the buildings of York.

Retrace your steps somewhat and bear left through a narrow passage next to the 'Hole in the Wall' and on to Precentor's Court. At the end of the road on the left notice the archway forming the entrance to the Purey Cust Nursing Home.

Petergate to which you enter is named after St. Peter, to whom the Minster is dedicated and is on the line of the Roman road - the Via Principalis. Indeed York's road structure can be said to be Roman, with the mediaeval street patterns imposed upon it and incorporated in it.

A city as old as York has its fair quota of myths and legends and the claim by the Hotel that Guy Fawkes was born there is a good example of this. We know from documentary evidence in the Minster Library that his parents lived at the other end of Stonegate where you saw the Plaque. (Of course Mrs. Fawkes might have slipped out for a shandy . . . .)

Fire Marks which you can see in High Petergate and elsewhere in the City are some 24 in number and date from the days

The Crosskeys of St. Peter and Arms of Dean Purey Cust.

The very attractive gates by Walker of York, (1837) beyond which lies the Dean's Park (Don't be distracted by this tranquil oasis however, there is still much to see and do !)

when if you insured your house the insurance company gave you one of these nice plaques and indeed some companies, notably The Sun Insurance, actually gave the policy number. Each insurance company had its own fire brigade who, it is said, gave priority to those which were insured with that company, but how true that is I would not like to say.

The West Front of the Minster is certainly the windiest place in York and has been known for many years as Kill Canon Corner, although we don't think that it has in truth killed any.

The double gas light standard (still, you will observe, burning gas)

Enter the Minster by the door on the left. Once inside notice above and behind you (on the far side)

The mediaeval carving showing Samson wrestling with the lion whilst Delila is busy cutting off his hair.

Move to the centre of the nave and observe above some splendid roof bosses

The Nativity and The Story of Pentecost are just two of the bible stories told on the eight bosses.

Now move eastwards and high up on your right notice

Stained Glass (12th century) telling the story of St. Nicholas

The Gas Lamps round the Minster have been maintained by the York Civic Trust as a vivid reminder of an interesting stage in the public lighting of York's streets, from flaming torches, oil and gas, to electricity. The lamp standards and the gates nearby - and indeed most of the old gas standards and railings in York - were made by a York firm called Walker, who made the huge and imposing railings outside the British Museum and the gates at the entrance to Kew Gardens. Walker became Royal Ironfounder to Queen Victoria, an honour you might think more rare than that of the Garter.

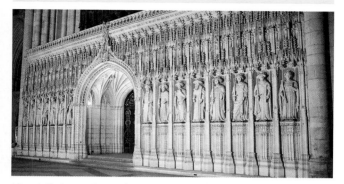

The full glory of the **Choir Screen (1473-1505)** depicting all the Kings of England from William I to Henry VI, seven on one side and eight on the other.

The Head of Henry IV with the dark stain that was put under the chin by the supporters of Archbishop Scrope whom the King had had executed.

The Minster is built on the sight of a former Norman Cathedral almost as big. It is the biggest mediaeval building, secular or religious, in England and took just over 250 years to build. It continues to dominate the City as it must have done even more markedly in mediaeval times. As you will have seen, it contains a wealth of stained glass (miraculously saved from the depredations of fire and two world wars) and also has a host of minor pleasures for the perceptive to enjoy. It is indeed an art gallery of stained glass of the highest quality which, with the various carvings, was a way of telling the Bible story to people who could not read or write. (For more information an excellent introduction is *Amy Oldfield's* book, The Stained Glass of York).

Attractive gilded stonework where you will see a cat chasing a mouse, which is well aware of the danger lurking.

Turn to the left and walking across the face of the Choir Screen, pass through the first set of gates

An interesting memorial to Lora, Viscountess Downe, whose character and *further particulars* may be seen in the Gentlemen's Magazine for May MDCCCXII (now sadly out of print).

Proceed along the aisle and enter St. Stephen's Chapel the

The attractive embroidered kneelers, depicting flowers of the world.

Carved reredos above the altar (by Street & Timworth, 1879) which depicts the Crucifixion.

The Roman Soldiers casting lots as to who should get Christ's robes. They have been given very Victorian moustaches.

The same soldiers dividing Christ's raiment between them, whilst to their right stands a little boy sucking his finger after plunging it into the jar of wine in front of him, and obviously enjoying it.

Exit to the left passing the

Great East Window (1405-8)

Turning right onto the South aisle look out for

The uncomfortable recumbent figure of Archbishop Hutton or has rigor mortis set in ? and a little further on the same side, notice the memorial to Jane Hodson who died in 1636. She was aged 38 having in that time had 24 children. She was the wife of a chancellor of the Minster, who has been described as being " an exceptionally active Chancellor" which you may well think to be the case. She certainly deserved a memorial.

At the end of the aisle turn left to the Tomb of Archbishop Walter de Grey, builder of the South Transept in 1220.

The walk around the Minster you have taken with this guide in your hands will have shown you that mediaeval man, despite his shortness of life and sternness of living, had a keen sense of humour. The nave roof bosses are copies of the mediaeval ones which were destroyed by a fire in 1829. Fortunately a York carver had drawn the original ones shortly before the fire and so was happy, as he says in his book, to hand these over to the then Dean 'before the ashes of the fire were cold'. But he reflects sadly how he never got any thanks or acknowledgement. Not the first man to feel the tooth of man's ingratitude. What is interesting is that the original mediaeval boss of the Nativity is said to portray Jesus being breast fed, but this was too much for the Victorians to bear and the present one shows him being fed from a bottle.

One of the embroidered kneelers depicting a Stylised peacock (a sign of the Resurrection) copied from an image used on the cushion which the Archbishop's head finally rested on.

Take advantage of the mobile mirrors to view the roof and window in the South Transept

The Rose Window showing the roses of York and Lancaster intertwined. The roof was restored after the disastrous fire of 1984.

Enter the regimental chapel on the right

West Yorkshire regiment (Prince of Wales' Own) served for many years in India and the colours each carry a figure of a tiger in various stages of fierceness, although this one looks more like a Cheshire cat.

Do return another day to explore the delights of this wonderful building but for now exit through the south door, noticing across the street

The very attractive rainwater head bearing the initials of
John Fountayne, Dean of York (1763), and his crest of an
elephant above.

*Follow the railings on the left to the rear of the Minster
passing the Red house and half-timbered St, William's College*

St. William's College which you see at the rear of the Minster
is certainly one of the finest and best preserved mediaeval
buildings in England. It was built by virtue of Letters Patent
granted by Warwick the Kingmaker, which phrase brings the
history you learnt in childhood back to life. You will have read
that it was built to house the chantry priests of the Minster and
this was for the very good reason that in most unseemly and
unpriestly fashion they had hitherto roamed the City streets at
night. Apart from its very fine timbered hall, it now houses an
attractive restaurant serving very wholesome meals.

Three men in a boat being blessed by the Bishop of Myra
and well they might be, because

The figure 50 feet above them is about to drop a cannon ball
onto the boat.

Retrace your steps to College Street and observe on the left

St. William's College built in 1465-7 to house the chantry
priests of the Minster. These were professional songmen paid
to sing masses for those who endowed them.

St. William himself was a nephew of William the
Conqueror.

*If time permits do go in and enjoy this very fine mediaeval
building and courtyard.*

*Now carry on down College Street and cross the road into
Goodramgate*

When you walked into Goodramgate you probably wondered
why most of the streets in York's historic core end their name
with the word 'gate'. This comes from 'gata', the
Scandinavian name for a road or a way, and is yet more
evidence of the Viking influence in York long after the
Romans had gone.

The attractive frosted glass incised window on the Cross Keys Public House

A short distance along this street brings you to

The oldest row of houses in York dating from 1316. (Don't look opposite at this generation's contribution to architecture).

Now enter through the iron gates at the side

The Churchyard of Holy Trinity on part of which the old houses were built. The church with its box pews, is one of the most delightful and charming churches in the City.

A fine (and rare) example of 15th century York glass. Notice also in the altar stone of the nearby chapel **one of its consecration crosses** polished by the fingers of countless modern day pilgrims.

*Having savoured the tranquillity of the church, return to
the street and proceed to the Old White Swan Public House.
If possible step into their courtyard and look out for*

Mounting Steps to enable the satisfied and possibly more than
satisfied customer to climb up on to his horse's saddle.

Return to the street, go right and carry on to the junction

Holy Trinity Church, first mentioned in 1082 but mainly of
the 14th and 15th centuries, lies behind the oldest row of
houses in York. It is one of the some twenty or so churches
surviving from the mediaeval times when there were no less
than forty two in the City. (Indeed it used to be said that there
was a church for every week in the year and a pub for almost
every day.) To go into that churchyard is to experience a
remarkable sense of tranquillity after the hustle and bustle of
the busy shopping street. Although now redundant, the
church is looked after by the Redundant Churches Fund
which ensures that it will be preserved intact for ever. The
very occasional church service is still held.

The pub next door to it, **The Old White Swan** with its
mounting steps goes back to mediaeval times and echoes the
days when York, having lost its pre-eminence in England, still
remained essentially a market town depending on the trade
which passed to and from the great agricultural plain of York
around it, and there is no doubt that this helped to sustain the
City until the coming of the nobility in the Georgian era and
the railway and chocolate still later. But it still to this day
retains its basic character as a market and county town.

Low Petergate with its classic view of the Minster towers beyond the mediaeval buildings.

Just a few yards into the street a **Little Red Indian.** The traditional sign of a Tobacconist's Shop. (There used to be one below).

Turn left into what is now known as King's Square (formerly the site of a Viking King's Palace) and pass along Colliergate to the end where you walk into York's shortest street.

Whip-Ma-Whop-Ma-Gate, mediaeval English for 'What a Street! Call this a Street?'

WHIP·MA·WHOP·MA·GATE

Notice the small church hall of St. Crux. Go in and see the monuments removed there from the church which formerly stood upon this site

One of the most attractive and well preserved mediaeval tombs in York.

Observe the chain round the neck of the recumbent **Sir Robert Watter who died in 1612.** This depicts the chain of office which he gave to the City and which is worn by Lord Mayors to this day.

When leaving the hall observe on your right York's oldest mediaeval Street

The Shambles derives its name from the Anglo-Saxon word shamel, meaning the stall or bench on which meat was displayed for sale. It's well worth walking up and down this unique street.

Turn back and proceed to the junction

The Thomas Herbert House. His grandson, Sir Thomas Herbert, accompanied Charles I on his way to the scaffold.

Now proceed to the right towards

All Saints, Pavement, the very fine guild church with its beautiful 15th century lantern tower.

The entrance is on the right of the Church

The streets around which you have walked are very little different from what they were in mediaeval times, having survived - owing to a number of influences - until the present day. The whole of the historic core of York is now a conservation area with little risk of it being spoilt by depredation and demolitions or the modernistic architecture of the 1960's which, with one or two notable exceptions, left the City unscathed. So it is still today very much a mediaeval city, built on Roman and later Viking foundations, with its original ring of walls which, with its four great gateways, is unique in England.

24

The attractive 13th century knocker showing a devil eating a human.

The fascinating boss which appears to depict a globe of the world with cutlasses on each side.

Exiting from the church, turn left and follow the pedestrian signs to the Jorvik Viking Centre and then to Fairfax House (N.B. disabled access is possible with assistance from staff)

Fairfax House, one of the finest - and most beautifully restored - 18th century houses in the City and home to the Noel Terry Collection of Furniture, one of the finest collections of Georgian Furniture in England and valued today at well over £4 million.

A study of the history of York over the last 200 or more years illustrates vividly how public opinion has reacted sharply to any proposals (chiefly and sadly emanating from the City Council) to destroy its character. Each generation has thankfully produced a handful of men and women who were prepared to stand up and vociferously protect it.

The Saloon draped with scarlet damask on the walls.

A splendid cabinet of 1700 featured by John Bly on the *BBC TV Antiques Roadshow*.

A silver sauce boat by Frederick Kandler, 1747 on the dining table

On leaving Fairfax House, glance to your left

Clifford's Tower (1244) and beyond it the Castle Museum.
Certainly places of interest worth visiting during your stay in York.

But York is not simply a mediaeval city on Roman and Viking foundations. The nobility of the Georgian era, living mainly in the country areas surrounding the City, (and many of them descendants of William the Conqueror's Knights), saw York

But for now turn right up Castlegate and beyond to St. Michael's Church. A redundant church now operating as an attractive restaurant.

The converted interior of the church has been tastefully done.

Notice a **15th century panel** in the east window with its unusual jewels and halo.

When suitably refreshed turn left onto York's main shopping street and proceed up Coney Street to

The very attractive clock on the left hand side outside the church of St. Martin le Grand (or what is left of it - it was bombed during the 2nd World War).	**A figure known as The Little Admiral** who holds a cross staff: an early form of sextant. He survived the bombing in the splendid tradition of the boy who stood on the burning deck, etc.

as an alternative to London in which to build town houses and desport themselves during the winter months. And so York has a wealth of Georgian buildings, including the magnificent Assembly Rooms still intact and one of the earliest neo-classical buildings in Europe. Indeed it can safely be said that it is second only to the Minster in architectural importance.

But for town houses none can equal **Fairfax House** in Castlegate by John Carr of York which, superbly restored by the York Civic Trust, now houses a remarkable collection of Early English clocks in which most of the noted clockmakers of the late 17th and early 18th centuries are represented. There is also a very fine collection of silver as well as regular exhibitions on 18th century life in York.

A little further and we return to our starting point, the Mansion house. It has one of the finest collections of civic plate in the country.

A solid silver chamber pot with whistle by Marmaduke Best, 1672. One of the more unusual pieces in the Civic collection!

A rather splendid Doulton china W.C. in the private office of the town Clerk (an appointment to see and certainly to use might be rather difficult to obtain).

The passageway to the side leads to the Guildhall, restored after being bombed during the war. Next to it are the council offices.

There we may finish our walk but those with extra stamina can turn left onto Lendal and proceed to the Judges Lodgings Hotel

Head of Aesculapius, the Greek God of Medicine (the house was built by Dr. Wintringham 1718-25).

The splendid parapet showing the white rose of York, the lions of England and the cross keys of the diocese. The iron-work is by Thomas Page, designer of Westminster Bridge.

The attractive lamp standards

29

Coat of Arms of York and
V & A for Victoria and Albert
in whose reign the bridge
was built.

*Carry on over the bridge
then take the steps on the
right (resisting the urge to
walk the city walls for the
moment) and descend to
the road. This is a short
detour but well worth the
effort, so turn right and
follow the river south until
you come to York's finest
mediaeval church.*

All Saints, North Street It
has a magnificent collection
of early 15th century glass.

Act of Visiting the Sick a detail from the window depicting the six corporate acts of mercy. The old man in this panel appears in all the others - he was the donor of the window and perhaps thereby sought to guarantee himself a place in heaven.

On the north side a mediaeval man wearing glasses (a rare sight in stained glass)

Retrace your steps back to the bridge and walking up the slight incline to the junction, cross over.

The splendid Coat of Arms of the Railway Company.
York does not consist entirely entirely of ancient buildings.
This headquarters of the N.E.R. railway company (1900 - 1961),
pictured below, is worth more than a passing glance.

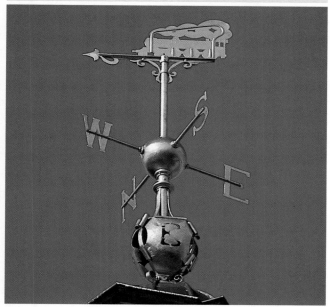

A fascinating weathervane with its puffing engine motif.

*Return to the road and pass through the lefthand arch
of the wall*

The cholera burial ground put deliberately *outside* the City
walls in 1832 to form the last resting place for the victims of
a plague of cholera.

*Now cross the road by the pedestrian crossing and head for
York's famous railway station.*

The Railway Station (or railway shed to use the parlance of
railway buffs) is a classic reminder of the era in York's history,
which saw the railway industry making a vital contribution to
the City's prosperity. It was George Hudson, one time Lord
Mayor of York, who swore that he would 'mak all t'railways
come to York' and he virtually succeeded in this aim, although
his methods of doing so led to his subsequent disgrace, penury
and death in Calais. But he had certainly left his mark upon the
City which has been an important Railway centre ever since.

The magnificent train shed 1871-77 which is 800 feet long with its dramatic roof curved to follow the lines below. It was aptly described by a distinguished art historian as York's propylaeum (you can buy a dictionary at the bookstall).

The spandrels of the arches on the top of the fine Corinthian columns depicting the Coats of Arms of the three companies which joined together to form the North Eastern Railway Company.

The coming of the chocolate industry, Terry's in the late 18th century and Rowntree's in the 19th century, set the seal on York's prosperity and gave it an economic stability. This foundation has enabled York to survive all the vicissitudes of two world wars and several major depressions. Nor has the City grown to an extent which would destroy its sense of identity. It today has a population, including the surrounding areas, of something over 100,000 people, amongst whom there is a strong sense of affinity with the City. It was Sir Harry Lauder, the Scots comedian who used to sing that 'I belong to Glasgow and Glasgow belongs to me'. And I think the same kinship is prevalent in York today and not just confined to two drinks on a Saturday night, as the Glaswegian was.

The Company's Initials may also be seen under some of the signal gantries. The station is one of the finest examples in England of Victorian railway engineering and a study of its many delights will amply repay the effort.

Now to be superseded by the channel tunnel! (but in truth the lettering was placed there for a scene in the film 'Chariots of Fire').

Our tour of some of the Minor Pleasures of York ends here but I'm sure you will have noticed throughout our journey that there is much more to explore and savour. Other walking guides in this Series may help you to do this and will be available in most good bookshops as and when they are published.

So as you leave the City, having spent, as you will realise by now, far too short a time in it to explore its treasures and pleasures fully, you can reflect on the fact that for a short time you have been in a city which - if not quite embodying the history of England, as George VI said - at least is a very good index to it, as a later historian wrote. Indeed successive tides of English history have ebbed and flowed against its walls and it has survived into the 20th century largely unscathed by wars and economic upheavals. In truth, a rich kaleidoscope of the architecture of all ages: a City where you can walk where the Romans, Normans and Vikings have gone before, a City which, as you walk around its narrow streets with your children or grandchildren, enables you to turn once again the pages of the history of England which you read in your childhood. A City to savour indeed.
And so we say au revoir, for certain it is that you will wish to return again and again.

YORK CIVIC TRUST

Patron: H.R.H. THE DUCHESS OF KENT

President: HIS GRACE THE ARCHBISHOP OF YORK

Chairman: JOHN SHANNON, O.B.E., D.UNIV. (YORK)

Registered Charity No. 229336

AIMS:

The Trust was established in 1946 with the object of preserving the City's rich architectural heritage, enhancing its amenities and encouraging good design in all fields.

It has found new uses for four medieval redundant churches; acquired and restored four buildings of great architectural and historic interest; affixed plaques to commemorate different facets of York's history; floodlit York Minster and many other churches and buildings; made grants to encourage works of conservation and to acquire various works of art.

Its Academic Development Committee was the progenitor of the University of York.

If you wish to know more about the work of the York Civic Trust and are considering membership,

please call in or write to:

Fairfax House
Castlegate
York YO1 1RN.
Tel: (0904) 655543
Fax: (0904) 652262